Potatoes

This book has been reviewed
for accuracy by
Jerry Doll
Professor of Agronomy
University of Wisconsin—Madison.

Library of Congress Cataloging in Publication Data

Pohl, Kathleen.
  Potatoes.

  (Nature close-ups)
  Adaptation of: Jagaimo / Hidetomo Oda.
  Summary: Takes a scientific look at the potato,
examining how it grows and reproduces.
  1. Potatoes—Juvenile literature. [1. Potatoes]
I. Oda, Hidetomo. Jagaimo. II. Title. III. Series.
QK495.S7P64   1986   583′.79   86-26239

ISBN 0-8172-2723-7 (lib. bdg.)
ISBN 0-8172-2741-5 (softcover)

This edition first published in 1987 by Raintree Publishers Inc.

Text copyright © 1987 by Raintree Publishers Inc., translated by
Jun Amano from *Potatoes* copyright © 1984 by Hidetomo Oda.

Photographs copyright © 1984 by Hidekazu Kubo.

World English translation rights for *Color Photo Books on Nature*
arranged with Kaisei-Sha through Japan Foreign-Rights Center.

1 2 3 4 5 6 7 8 9 0   90 89 88 87 86

Potatoes

Adapted by
Kathleen Pohl

Raintree Publishers
Milwaukee

◄ Baking potatoes.

There are more than 5,000 kinds of potatoes in the world. Russet Burbank is the most popular baking potato in the United States.

► A field of potatoes.

Potatoes need sunshine, lots of rain, and warm days and cool nights in order to grow well.

Baked potatoes, french fries, potato salad, potato chips. Almost everyone has eaten the potato in one form or another. The popular vegetable is grown in many parts of the world. In some countries, potatoes are also used as cattle feed and in making alcohol and flour.

Potatoes were first grown in South America more than 400 years ago. The Incas planted potatoes high up in the Andes Mountains. They made a light, powdery flour from the potatoes and used it for baking bread.

Spanish explorers brought potatoes back to Europe from South America in the mid-1500s. From there, potatoes spread throughout Europe. And when the Pilgrims landed at Plymouth Rock in 1620, they carried potato seeds with them to the new land.

► Potato salad.

Potatoes can be prepared in a variety of ways. Some are processed as chips or flakes. Others are used fresh, in salads, soups, or casseroles.

◀ **Cross-section of a potato.**

Most of the potato is water. The pith, the inner part of the potato, holds most of the water. The starch is stored in the outer area of cells, called the cortex.

▶ **Pieces of starch stored in cells.**

When you brush iodine on a cut potato, you can see the starchy areas as they turn blue.

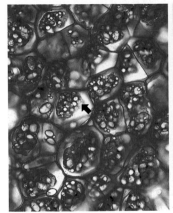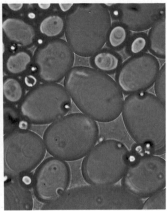

Stored starch in cells.   Enlarged grains of starch.

The part of the potato plant that people eat is called the tuber. It grows underground and is where the potato plant stores its extra food, which is called starch. Potatoes also contain calcium, some vitamins, and protein—all of which have important food value for people—and for potato plants. In fact, the potato has been called one of nature's most perfect foods.

To see where the starch is stored in the potato, cut one in half with a knife. Then, with help from an adult, brush some iodine onto the potato's cut surface. Watch as the white part of the potato turns blue-black. That is where the starch is stored, in tiny plant units, called cells.

But most of the tuber—about 80 percent of it—is water, which you can see if you grate a potato.

◀ **Extracting starch from a potato.**

Grate a potato to make a fine pulp. Wrap the grated potato in a piece of cloth and pour water through it. Then squeeze out the remaining water. In a few minutes, the white starch will settle to the bottom of the glass.

▶ **Add iodine to the starch.**

Add a drop or two of iodine to the starch. Watch as it turns blue-black.

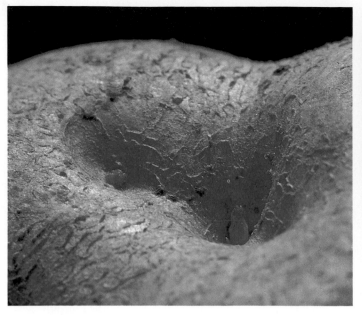

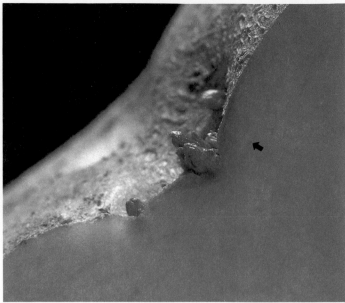

▲ **New buds growing in the eyes of a potato.**

When a potato is taken out of cold storage, buds begin to grow. Soon sprouts develop from the tiny buds.

▲ **A cross-section of a potato's eye.**

Food and water are carried to all parts of the potato plant through a network of veins, called vascular bundles (arrow).

Once potatoes are dug out of the ground, they should be stored in a cool place. If the temperature in the storage area is too warm, the potatoes will soon begin to sprout. Sprouts are new shoots that develop from tiny potato buds. If you look closely at the sprouting potato, you will notice that the buds and sprouts grow wherever there are little dents on the potato's surface. These are called eyes.

Instead of planting potatoes from true seeds, people usually cut up potato tubers and plant the pieces. Each piece of seed potato must have an eye so that buds can form and sprout. Then new plants can develop.

◀ **The top and bottom of a potato (left) and the potato's bottom, with its dead stem (right).**

Like other vegetables, the potato has a top and bottom side. You can find the bottom by looking for the largest dent with the dead stem.

▼ A sprouting potato. Potatoes sprout at about 70°F. These sprouts are already developing tiny green leaves. The sprouts are nourished by the stored starch and protein inside the potato.

◄ **A man planting potatoes.**

Because they grow best in cool weather, potatoes are planted in the spring in the northern United States, and during winter in the southern states.

► **A potato growing underground.**

Long thin roots grow first from the base, then along the sides of the sprouts. The tips of the sprouts form the leaves of the new potato plant.

Once a seed potato is planted in the ground, its sprouts begin to develop into the roots and stems of the new potato plant. From the tips of the sprouts, the tiny green leaves of the new plant will form.

At first, the growing plant is nourished by the starch and protein stored inside the seed potato. But soon the new plant's roots spread out in many directions. They become covered with fine hairs. When the seed potato's nutrients have been all used up, the root hairs reach out into the nearby soil. They begin to take in water and nutrients for the new young potato plant.

▼ **Potato roots.**

Roots grow outward from their tips. They are protected by tiny root caps as they push through the soil.

▼ **Roots with root hairs.**

The root hairs absorb water and nutrients from the soil. They do not live long and are found only on the newest part of the root.

▲ **A potato plant pushing through the soil.**

When the ground temperature reaches 60°F, the plants emerge aboveground in the spring.

▲ **Leaves of a potato plant.**

The leaves of potatoes and other plants are green because they contain chlorophyll.

Potatoes grow best where average temperatures are mild, about 60° to 70°F. It takes three to four months for potato plants to produce mature potatoes.

The plant's roots and stem develop underground. The roots grow down into the soil. The leaves form at the tips of the sprouts. They are well formed by the time they push their way through the top soil. The leaves get their green color from a coloring matter, or pigment, called chlorophyll. The thick, green leaves play an important part in the potato plant's development. The tiny cells in the plant leaves provide food for the growing potato plant.

◄ **Potato leaves growing at the tip of a sprout.**

At first, the leaves overlap one another, like tiny fish scales (left photo). As they grow, the small leaves seem to wrap themselves around the tip of the sprout (right photo).

▼ Potato plants growing underground, nourished by seed potatoes.

The potato stems grow rapidly underground. They are nourished by the seed potato's stored energy. As the stems reach toward the surface and receive sunlight, the leaves turn green.

▲ Young potato leaves.

At first, the leaves are round and simple. Later, they develop more leaflets and become compound leaves.

▲ Compound leaves.

At this stage of growth, the seed potato's stored food has been used up. The plant's leaves now produce food for the growing plant.

Potato plants, like all green plants, make food for themselves through a complex process called photosynthesis. Photosynthesis means "to produce with light." During this process, green plants combine energy from sunlight with carbon dioxide and water to produce food. It is the plant's green leaves which absorb sunlight, making it possible for photosynthesis to take place.

The food produced by the potato plant is called glucose. It is necessary for the plant's growth. Glucose is carried to all parts of the potato plant by a network of veins in the stem, called the vascular system.

Many insects like to feed on the tender, young leaves of the potato plant. Beetles, aphids, and potato bugs can all do a great deal of damage to potato crops.

◄ Potato plants folding up their leaves.

Young potato plants unfold their leaves during the day to receive sunlight, and fold them up at night. Mature plants don't fold up their leaves at night.

► Rows of thriving potato plants.

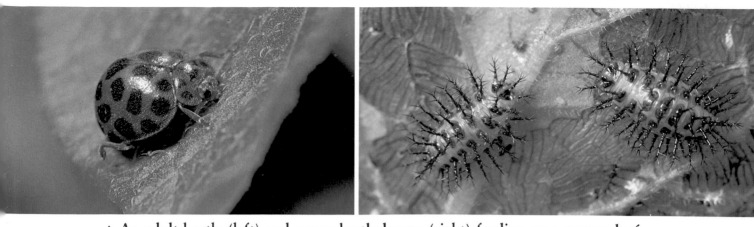

▲ An adult beetle (left) and young beetle larvae (right) feeding on a potato leaf.

▲ **Flower buds on a potato plant.**

Potato plants flower about two months after they are planted. The amount of time varies with the kind of plant and the weather conditions.

▲ **A flower bud swelling.**

If the air temperature is too warm—over 70°F—buds sometimes fail to bloom at all.

As the tubers develop underground, the potato plants begin to flower aboveground. The flowers vary in color, depending on the kind of potato. Some are white, others are pink or dark purple. The flowers are shaped like five-pointed stars and look like those of eggplant or tomato plants. Potatoes, tomatoes, and eggplants all belong to the same family, the Solanaceae family.

Flowers are important to plants because they produce seeds from which new plants grow. But not all potato plants have flowers. Some kinds never flower, and some flower only if the weather is right. Flowers are not as necessary to potato plants as they are to other plants because potatoes, as we have discussed, can reproduce by sprouting (tubers), as well as by flowering (seeds).

◄ **Flowers of the Solanaceae family.**

An eggplant flower (left) and tomato flower (right) are very similar to the flowers of the potato plant. The same kinds of insects, ladybugs and shield bugs, feed on different members of the Solanaceae family.

▼ Potato flowers blooming. The upper petals open first. The others follow, one after the other. Potato flowers die several days after they bloom.

▼ A potato field in flower. The male and female parts of a potato flower mature at different times. So potato plants often receive pollen from other plants. This is called cross-pollination.

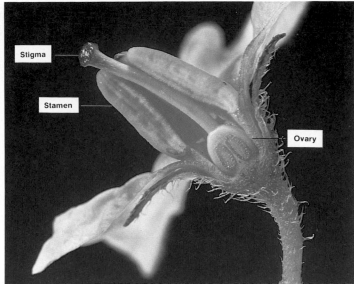

Stigma

Stamen

Ovary

▲ **A potato flower ready to be pollinated.**

Insects or the wind will carry pollen from another potato plant to the sticky tip of this plant's pistil. The tip is called the stigma.

▲ **A cross-section of a flower.**

The pollen grain sends a long tube down the pistil to the ovary. Then a sperm from the pollen grain joins with an egg, fertilizing it.

Potato flowers have both female and male parts. The female parts include the pistil, the ovary, and the eggs. Inside the petals is the pistil, which is a long, thick tube. At the base of the pistil is the ovary, where tiny female egg cells form.

The pistil is surrounded by five bright yellow stamens. These are the male parts of the flower. The stamens produce dustlike grains of pollen, which contain the male sperm cells. When a sperm joins with an egg, the egg becomes fertilized, and a plant seed soon begins to grow.

▶ **A cross-section of the five stamens surrounding the pistil.**

When the pollen is mature, it is released through tiny holes at the tips of the stamens.

◄ A dronefly on a potato plant.

Plant pollen sticks to the bodies of insects as they fly from plant to plant, searching for flower nectar. Droneflies seem to be especially attracted to potato plants.

► A potato fruit developing (photos 1-4).

Some potato plants produce fruits. After the pollinated flowers have died, the ovaries develop into green fruits. They look like young tomatoes.

Potato plants don't usually self-pollinate. They usually become pollinated when pollen is carried from one plant to another by insects or the wind. This is called cross-pollination.

Once a grain of pollen lands on the stigma of the pistil, it sends a long tube down the pistil. The sperm cells travel down the tube and join with the eggs in the ovary.

The potato flower soon withers, but the fertilized seeds begin to grow inside the ovary. The ovary forms a hard, protective covering around the seeds. When the potato fruit has formed, it looks very much like a small, green tomato.

► Ripe potato fruits.

◄ Seeds inside a potato fruit.

If you cut a potato fruit open, you can see its seeds. While potato plants can be grown from potato tubers, new varieties of potatoes can only be developed from seeds.

21

◀ **A view of the underground part of potato plants.**

After the flowers die, the potato plants don't grow much bigger aboveground. Most of the extra glucose produced by the leaves is carried underground, and changed into starch, to be stored. The potatoes grow rapidly as the supply of starch increases.

▶ **New potatoes and a decayed seed potato.**

Once all the nutrients from the seed potato have been used up, it withers and dies. The new potatoes now store food and water for the plant.

Potato plants are most active during the flowering season. The large green leaves produce nutrients that are carried to other parts of the plant by the vascular bundles. The plant produces more food than it can use. The excess food is taken to a part of the plant that extends underground, called the stolon. The stolons look like roots, but they serve as a special place for storing food. As extra food is stored in the stolons, their tips begin to swell. This stored food is called starch, and it forms most of the tuber, the potato which we eat.

▶ **Potatoes that have turned green.**

If potatoes are exposed to sunshine as they grow, they turn green and are bitter-tasting. So farmers "hill" potatoes—pile up dirt at the base of the plant to keep the tubers covered as they grow. In the left photo are green potatoes. In the right photo, a green potato is sprouting.

◀ **A potato field where leaves have begun to change color.**

Several months after flowering, the leaves of these potato plants begin to wither.

▶ **Full-grown potatoes that have just been harvested.**

Potatoes grown in the United States are usually brown, red, or white. Potatoes in other countries sometimes have deep purple or black skins.

A month or two after the flowering season, the leaves of the potato plant turn yellow. By this time, the underground potatoes have grown very large. But before the plant's stems and leaves die completely, the potatoes absorb their remaining nutrients.

Large fields of potatoes are harvested by machines, and smaller ones are often harvested by hand. It is easier to dig up the potatoes if the potato plant has died. In the fall, frost often kills potato plants, making it easier for the potatoes to be harvested.

Usually, there are three to six edible potatoes on a plant, but there may be as many as ten or twenty. The number depends on the variety of potato and on the growing conditions. Some potatoes grow more than six inches long and weigh as much as three pounds. But most are much smaller.

● **A potato stolon stained with colored water.**

If a potato stolon takes up colored water, it will absorb the color (left). The color is carried to the rest of the potato by the vascular system. The arrow in the photo at the right shows a vascular bundle that has absorbed the red coloring.

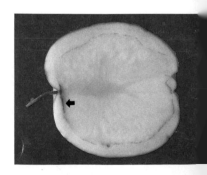

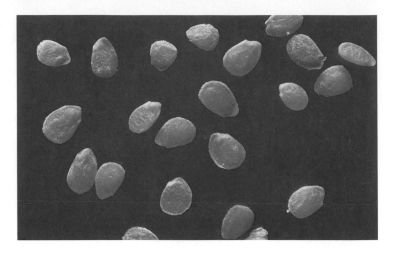

◀ **Potato seeds.**

These tiny potato seeds have just enough stored food to nourish seed leaves in a new plant.

▶ **A stolon developing at the base of a seedling stem (photos 1-3).**

Potato plants grown from seeds develop stolons at the base of their seed leaves. Small potatoes develop at the ends of the stolons.

Potato plants can be grown from true seeds as well as from tubers, or seed potatoes. But it takes much longer for potato plants to develop from seeds. Seed potatoes can store more nutrients than seeds can. So the new plants get a headstart when they are planted from tubers.

But new varieties of potatoes can be produced only if the plants are grown from true seeds. A plant grown from a seed potato is an exact copy of the seed potato plant. Plants grown from true seeds, however, combine characteristics of two different parent plants. And that is how new varieties are formed. Over the years, many new kinds of potatoes have been developed. Some are good for baking; others are best in salads. Some kinds are even specially grown to be made into potato chips.

▼ **Seedlings.**

The newly planted seeds must be watered often. Gradually, the stems extend and the seed leaves open up.

▼ **True leaves growing between seed leaves.**

True leaves grow from nourishment provided by the seed leaves. This potato plant is still just an inch high.

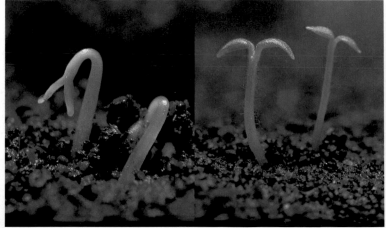

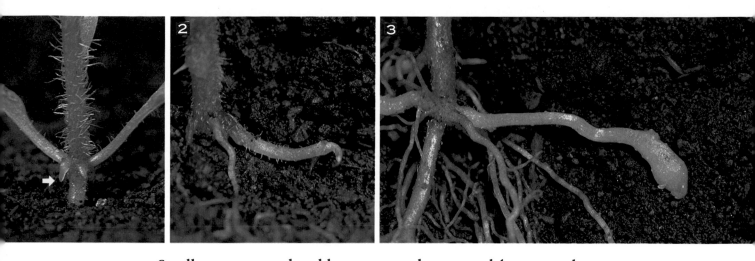

▼ Small potatoes produced by a potato plant started from a seed.

◄ **A potato field at harvest-time.**

This harvesting machine digs potatoes out of the ground, shakes the dirt off them, and loads the potatoes into a nearby truck.

▶ **A truckload of harvested potatoes.**

Once they have been harvested, the potatoes are loaded onto trucks. Some are hauled to storage bins, others to grocery stores.

By the time potatoes have grown large enough to harvest, thick skins have formed on the starchy tubers. There are tiny buds in the eyes of the potato, ready to sprout into life.

Once the potatoes are harvested, some are kept in storage. Some are processed into potato chips, frozen french fries, or hashbrowns, and are shipped to grocery stores. And some will be used for seed potatoes for next year's crop.

Whether you dig your own potatoes out of the ground or buy them at a grocery store, they should be stored in a cool place until you are ready to use them. A good storage temperature is 40° to 50°F. If the temperature is higher, the potatoes will soon begin to sprout. If it is lower, the starch in the potatoes will turn to sugar, and you will notice a sweet taste when you eat them.

Round baron potatoes. Long Mayqueen potatoes.

◄ **Potatoes have different flavors, depending on the variety.**

Different kinds of potatoes have different flavors, depending on the amount of starch that is stored in the tuber, and the size of the starch grains.

Let's Find Out How to Raise Potatoes.

Use a flower pot at least eight inches across to give your plant plenty of room to grow.

Potato plants are easy to grow. Try growing plants in a large flower pot or wooden box. The green stems and leaves of the potato plant need sunshine to produce tubers. So place your flower pot where it will get lots of sunlight.

Cut potatoes into fairly large pieces. Make sure each piece has an eye.

■ How to Grow Potatoes

Place soil in a container. Dig a hole three inches deep and place a piece of potato, with the eye up, in the hole. If you plant more than one potato, place them about a foot apart.

When a sprout is about to come out of the ground, add two inches of soil. When the sprouts become two to three inches long, pick them all off except for a few good sprouts.

Be sure to water your plant. During the flowering season, add two inches more soil so the potatoes won't be exposed to sunshine. Water the plants less as harvest-time nears.

Raising Potatoes

Place a cut potato in a dish or tray with water. It may grow stems, and flowers may bloom. At the base of the stems, you may see stolons form. Place one dish or tray in a sunny place and one in the shade. See how the potatoes differ in their rates of growth.

A potato seed piece kept in the dark.

Stems with leaves formed on seed piece placed in light.

Seed Potatoes

The idea of using seed potatoes originated in the United States. Growing potatoes from tubers, rather than seeds, cuts down the growing time.

A plant from a seed.

Potatoes from a seed.

Sunshine and Photosynthesis

Cover part of a leaf with a piece of aluminum foil for a half a day. After boiling the leaf in water for one minute, discolor it in alcohol. When iodine is added to the leaf, the part that was covered with aluminum foil does not turn purple. Photosynthesis, which produces sugars and starches, cannot take place without sunlight.

A leaf covered with foil.

An iodine test.

A Potato Is a Kind of Stem.

Potatoes develop at the end of stolons. If stolons are taken out of the ground and exposed to the sun, they turn green. And if young potatoes are taken out of the ground and exposed to the sun, their skins turn green. This shows that potatoes are extensions of the plant stem, used as storage areas.

A stolon above ground.

Green potatoes.

GLOSSARY

chlorophyll—the substance, or pigment, in plants that gives them their green color. (p. 12)

glucose—a kind of sugar produced during photosynthesis which is used as food by the potato plant. (p. 14)

ovary—the base of the pistil of a flower, where the eggs develop. (pp. 19, 20)

photosynthesis—the process by which green plants make food, with the help of chlorophyll and energy from sunlight. Photosynthesis occurs in the plant's leaves. (p. 14)

pistil—the female reproductive part of a plant. (pp. 19, 20)

pollen—the tiny grains that contain male sperm cells which fertilize the plant's eggs. (pp. 19, 20)

pollination—the process in which pollen is transferred from the stamen to the tip, or stigma, of the pistil. (pp. 18, 20)

stamen—the male reproductive part of a plant. (p. 19)

starch—the extra food stored by the potato plant. (pp. 7, 23)

tubers—the underground storage organs for the potato plant. Tubers are commonly called potatoes. (pp. 7, 16)